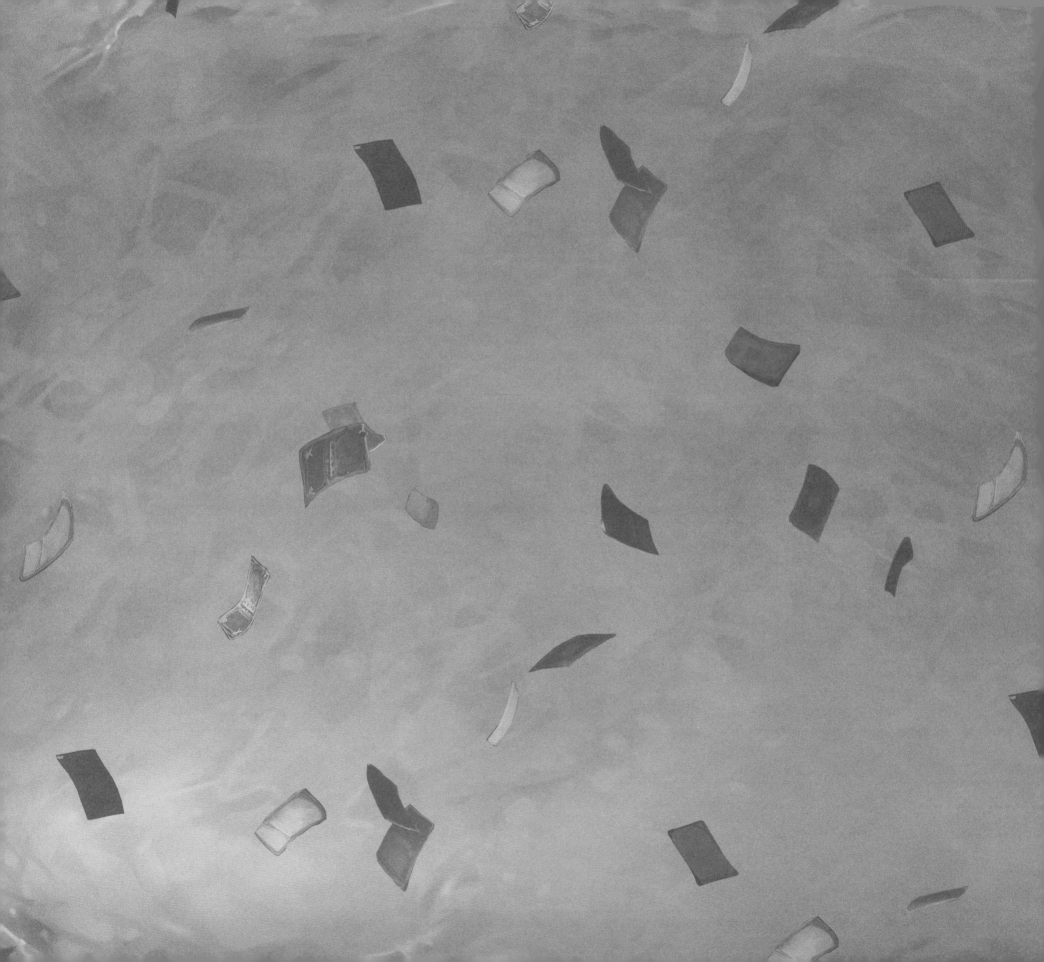

The Art of
HEARTHSTONE

Volume II:
Year of the Kraken

TITAN BOOKS

BLIZZARD ENTERTAINMENT

Editors: Allison Irons, Paul Morrissey
Game Team Direction: Jeremy Cranford, Ben Thompson
Creative Consultation: Jason Chayes, Dave Kosak
Lore Consultation: Sean Copeland, Christi Kugler,
Justin Parker
Production: Phillip Hillenbrand, Brianne M Loftis,
Timothy Loughran, Alix Nicholaeff,
Derek Rosenberg, Cara Samuelsen
Director, Consumer Products: Byron Parnell
Director, Creative Development: Ralph Sanchez and
David Seeholzer
Special Thanks: Wendy Campbell, Tim Erskine, Jerry
Mascho

DESIGN BY CAMERON + COMPANY

Publisher: Chris Gruener
Creative Director: Iain R. Morris
Art Director: Suzi Hutsell
Designer: Rob Dolgaard

Published by Titan Books, London, in 2019.

TITAN BOOKS

A division of Titan Publishing Group Ltd
144 Southwark Street
London SE1 0UP
www.titanbooks.com

Find us on Facebook: www.facebook.com/titanbooks
Follow us on Twitter: @TitanBooks

A CIP catalogue record for this title is available from the
British Library.

ISBN: 9781789093506
Manufactured in China

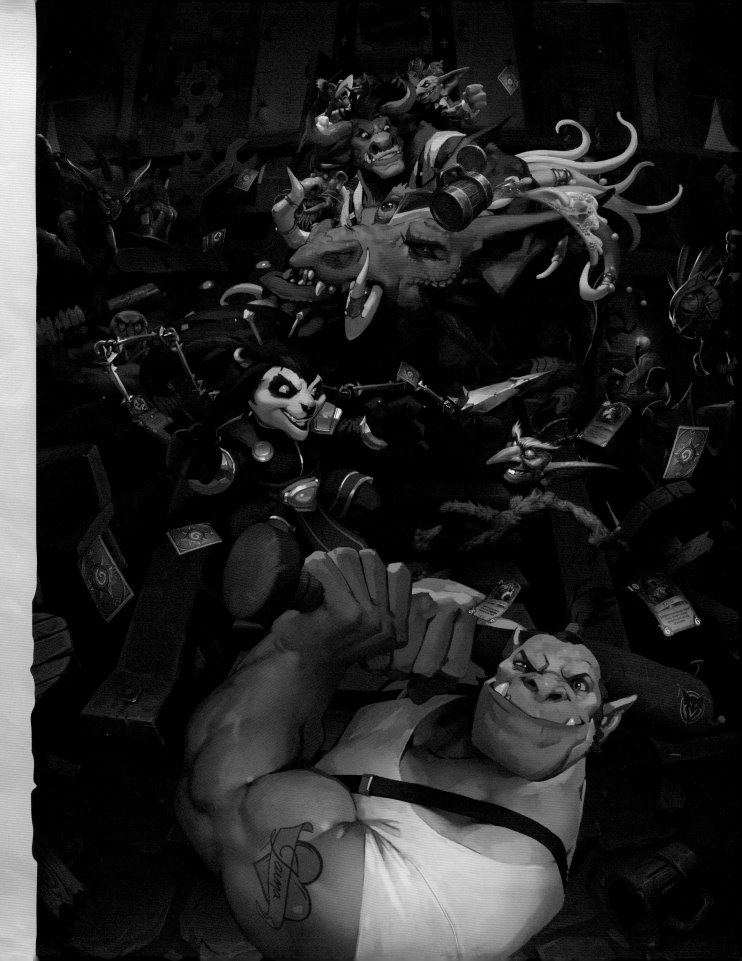

CONTENTS

INTRODUCTION:
Ringing in the New Year

As the people of Azeroth sleep, the night sky watches over them. Endless legions of stars peek out of the darkness, winking, forming a shimmering curtain across the cosmos.

There are portents up there in the sky, you know. Look closely, and you'll learn secrets about things that were, things that are, and things that will be. One night, years ago, I sensed a change. The stars did not move, yet I saw them aligning into a new pattern.

And on that night, I saw two menacing eyes peering out at me not from the sky, but the depths of an ocean so deep no light could touch it.

The kraken was stirring. It was coming for me. I could feel it in my bones.

I tell ya, I couldn't have been more excited! It's always a treat to have a little adventure in your life.

—Harth Stonebrew, the Innkeeper

RIGHT

Charlene Le Scanff and Jomaro Kindred

By the start of 2016, *Hearthstone* had grown from a passion project to a global phenomenon. The development team for Blizzard Entertainment's digital collectible card game (CCG) had already shipped hundreds of cards in two full expansions and three adventures, bringing new faces, new mechanics, and a never-ending stream of new art to the millions upon millions of people who had flocked to Azeroth's friendliest tavern.

"That was about the time we knew that we needed to make some changes," said art director Ben Thompson. "Sure, we were proud of the work we had done, but all of that was just the beginning, right? How was the game going to change over the next year, and the years beyond it?"

A new game mode had already been introduced. The very first Tavern Brawls—time-limited game modes featuring unusual rule sets and scenarios—had launched in 2015 and would become an important part of the team's plans in the coming year.

The competitive scene had also been revamped. In 2016, a new championship tour format was unveiled, splitting the year into three seasons. At the end of the year, the highest performing players would come to Anaheim to battle for the title of global champion at BlizzCon. The 2016 winner, Russian player Pavel Beltiukov, took home the trophy and $250,000 for his victory.

Even the development team itself had changed. As any innkeeper knows, when the common room gets crowded, you have to bring on some additional hosts to keep the good times rolling. The small internal Hearthstone team had grown by dozens, and the legion of freelance artists was always adding new members to its ranks.

All of these changes were in preparation for the biggest transformation the game had seen yet: The core game mode of *Hearthstone* was about to be split in two . . .

ABOVE
Hearthstone Championship Tour logo

OPPOSITE
Hearthstone Global Games logo and sketches

1

CHANGING OF THE SEASONS

Let's make magic!

—Cult Sorcerer

I n February 2016, the development team announced the introduction of Standard format, the new core game mode for competitive play. The basic cards, the classic sets, and the cards from the previous two calendar years would be eligible for use. The others would rotate out of play. A brand-new mode, Wild format, would be the place where every card from *Hearthstone*'s entire history could be played.

From a design standpoint, the split between Standard and Wild was absolutely necessary. *Hearthstone*'s designers and developers had known for a long time that "power creep" could become a real danger as the years passed. Eventually, certain cards and meta archetypes would become so powerful that the only way to give players a chance to fight back would be to design even more powerful cards, which could then only be countered by more power cards . . .

It was a lesson other card games had learned the hard way. Standard format narrowed the focus of competitive play, allowing powerful archetypes to come and go on a neat schedule. It also allowed new players—who are inherently at a disadvantage with an empty collection in a CCG—to spend their precious gold on a smaller array of card packs. And, hopefully, it would create excitement for the new cards that would come each year

While standard format had some great advantages, there remained potential for problems. The main hurdle would be to communicate these changes to the players. A player who took a year off from the game would be bewildered when all their old decks weren't eligible for competitive play, and any player who didn't pay attention to blog posts and Twitter feeds would feel blindsided when the new year arrives and their collection is thrown into disarray.

The development team worked to minimize these issues long before the format split was announced. Countless user interface and design tweaks were implemented to allow players to sort through their cards by expansion and format.

And, of course, the art team put their noses to the grindstone. In the early prototyping days of *Hearthstone*, the power and value of artistic design had been proven many times over. Many mechanics were made intuitive (and sometimes technically stunning) because of clever and dramatic visual cues.

What if a new player hasn't seen **Divine Shield** before? Once they see how it pops up like a protective bubble before taking damage, its purpose is easy to understand. If they didn't read **Sylvanas Windrunner**'s card text too closely? After a couple instances of seeing her shadowy tendrils reach out, curving in unpredictable directions before snatching its target, they'll understand that her **Deathrattle** effect will randomly steal an enemy minion.

The key to the visual design for the format change had little to do with cards, but rather with the overall aesthetic inside the game itself. If the Standard format was going to be predicated on calendar years, then the "Hearthstone new year" should be a momentous event, heralded with anticipation, excitement, and celebration like how most real-world cultures celebrate the new year.

LEFT
Will Muray

Thinking through those lines led to an interesting idea. Many ancient cultures developed their calendar systems by studying the stars. They found patterns, noticed shapes among the stars, and observed that everything seemed to repeat every twelve months or so.

"The idea of showing the Tavern's new year through our own zodiac calendar felt awesome," said Jeremy Cranford, one of Hearthstone's art managers. "We could write the history of our game in the stars. Oh, yeah. I liked that a lot."

After much debate, the first Standard year was announced: The Tavern was about to ring in the **Year of the Kraken**.

As every player logged into the game for the first time in the new year, they were treated to an animation showing an elaborate, ornate clock clicking and rumbling to life, revealing the icon of a menacing kraken, tentacles and all.

"Why the kraken? It was otherworldly, but recognizable motif," said Ben Thompson. "We needed something that felt like the changing of the year, and we didn't want to choose an animal that might feel like it was from an annual zodiac calendar that already exists on Earth. Also, it was a perfect fit for our first expansion of the year."

That icon became the sigil of the entire year, marking the different expansions and adventure, as well as the competitive gaming tournaments for 2016.

And yes, it did fit in quite well for the first expansion of the year; it was the release that would welcome both the new year and an ancient darkness into the Tavern . . .

ABOVE
Hearthstone astrological clock

OPPOSITE
Hearthstone astrological clock sketches

2

WHISPERS OF THE OLD GODS™

Your deck betrays you.

—C'THUN

DEFINING EVIL

The first release of the Year of the Kraken was unquestionably the darkest *Hearthstone* expansion thus far. Heralded by a mysterious troll seer with a penchant for corruption, *Whispers of the Old Gods* immediately tainted the meta with its twisted minions, enslaved creatures, and soul-shattering powers.

The four Old Gods themselves emerged from their lairs of evil as key cards in powerful new deck archetypes. **C'Thun** became a ticking time bomb of destruction, always lurking in the corner of both players' eyes as its dreaming came to an end. **N'Zoth** resurrected an army of dead minions to fight at its side. **Y'Shaarj** made sure to invite its biggest and deadliest friends every time it stepped onto the board. And **Yogg-Saron**, praise be its randomness, was the ultimate force of indiscriminately applied annihilation—so much so that within a few months it had to be put on a leash. (There is such a thing as too much corruption, apparently.)

The four whispering avatars of evil were always destined to be the lynchpins of their decks, and that meant they needed appropriately awesome and threatening card art.

That was going to be a challenge, because only **C'Thun** and **Yogg-Saron** had even been seen in *World of Warcraft*. Y'Shaarj had some stained-glass-style windows made in its honor once, but that was it. In 2016, **N'Zoth** was a complete mystery.

PREVIOUS PAGE
Laurel Austin

RIGHT
Even Amundsen

So, for **Y'Shaarj** and **N'Zoth**, Hearthstone artists had the chance—and the responsibility—to define how they would look. Forever.

"We knew we couldn't just do what we wanted. *Warcraft* players were going to see them for the first time too," said Jeremy Cranford. "However we showed **N'Zoth** and **Y'Shaarj**, that was going to be how people remembered them."

Hearthstone artists huddled together with other concept artists and illustrators across the company, including the Warcraft team. After sketching out countless iterations, the team finally assembled their Old God gallery. The key in differentiating their looks was to choose which strange, disturbing features to highlight for each one.

C'Thun's art focused on his massive, all-seeing eye, looming like a tower above the land. **Yogg-Saron**'s art highlighted his half-submerged, half-open, eternally screaming maw with dozens of smaller mouths across his face howling in unison.

Y'Shaarj's art used an almost symmetrical composition to highlight his twisted face and head. And **N'Zoth**, the great unknown creature, was portrayed as a nightmarish beast of the sea, rising above the waves with countless tentacles reaching to ensnare anything nearby.

The Old Gods were ready to play. And they were bringing a wicked crowd with them.

Now I've got a tale to tell you of the ones from long ago . . .

—MADAME LAZUL

LEFT
Grzegorz Przybyś and Laurel Austin

*You can lock your doors,
you can say your prayers;
no creature can resist
their wicked words.*

—Madame Lazul

LEFT
Arthur Bozonnet

29

FAMILIAR, YET DIFFERENT —AND SUPER EVIL

Evil can be represented in a million different visual ways. "And that's a problem if we're trying to find a consistent look," said Ben Thompson. "The key to defining the style of the expansion set was to show what something familiar would look like after the Old Gods got their tentacles on it."

After a few weeks of experimentation and iteration, development team artists created a foundational image that was relatively simple: It showed what a bear from **Azeroth** looked like before and after becoming corrupted by the Old Gods.

"It's corrupted. That's the key word," said Jeremy Cranford. "It doesn't have evil-looking armor on top of a normal body. Its flesh is being transformed at a cellular level. And the transformation isn't done yet. You're seeing the transition between normal and 'Old God,' and it's a freaky middle ground to be in."

It was a process that had been used in previous expansions. *The Grand Tournament* had applied the lens of the medieval-style knight in shining armor to all sorts of strange creatures. What does a murloc knight ride into a joust? (A frog!) What does an orc pirate ride? (A parrot, of course!) It's a way to spark the imagination of a wide group of artists while making sure nobody wanders too far off target.

The Hearthstone team looked through a lens of disturbing transformations for the *Whispers of the Old Gods* release, too, but not just for the art illustrations. Familiar card mechanics and even a beloved game board were twisted and corrupted to show the effect the Old Gods were having on the Tavern.

One of the first game boards in *Hearthstone* was the Stormwind board. But for this expansion, a new version was created—one where the cathedral in the corner had eyes instead of windows and the friendly gryphon in another corner had putrid, fleshy wings.

ABOVE
Wooden expansion sign

RIGHT
Whispers of the Old Gods
logo ideation and final logo

Uncorrupted

Many of the cards in the set were altered versions of recognizable minions. Cards like **Loot Hoarder** and **Amani Berserker** were transformed into the red-eyed and tentacle-laden **Polluted Hoarder** and **Aberrant Berserker**.

"We had **King Mukla** in the classic set, so we created a corrupted version (**Mukla, Tyrant of the Vale**) for this set. For the people who know what he looked like, the difference tells the story about what the Old Gods' corruption does to you," said Cranford. "And if you've never seen that old card in your life, you still know, 'Something is wrong with that gorilla.'"

After defining the look of corruption, the team moved on to determining what the loyal servants of the Old Gods would look like. There were the inhuman Faceless Ones, (or n'raqi, for you lore fiends) who are the Void-spawned minions of the Old Gods, and there were also the cultists working to enact their masters' will.

C'Thun's followers had the most distinctive designs because they were the only minions with a direct mechanical connection to their Old God. Cards like **C'Thun's Chosen** and **Disciple of C'Thun** had prominent designs of **C'Thun**'s eye on their clothing to clearly mark their allegiance, and their voice lines often mentioned **C'Thun** by name.

ABOVE
Sunny Gho

RIGHT
Tyson Murphy

Corrupted

ABOVE
Whispers of the Old Gods game board sketch

OPPOSITE
Final *Whispers of the Old Gods* game board

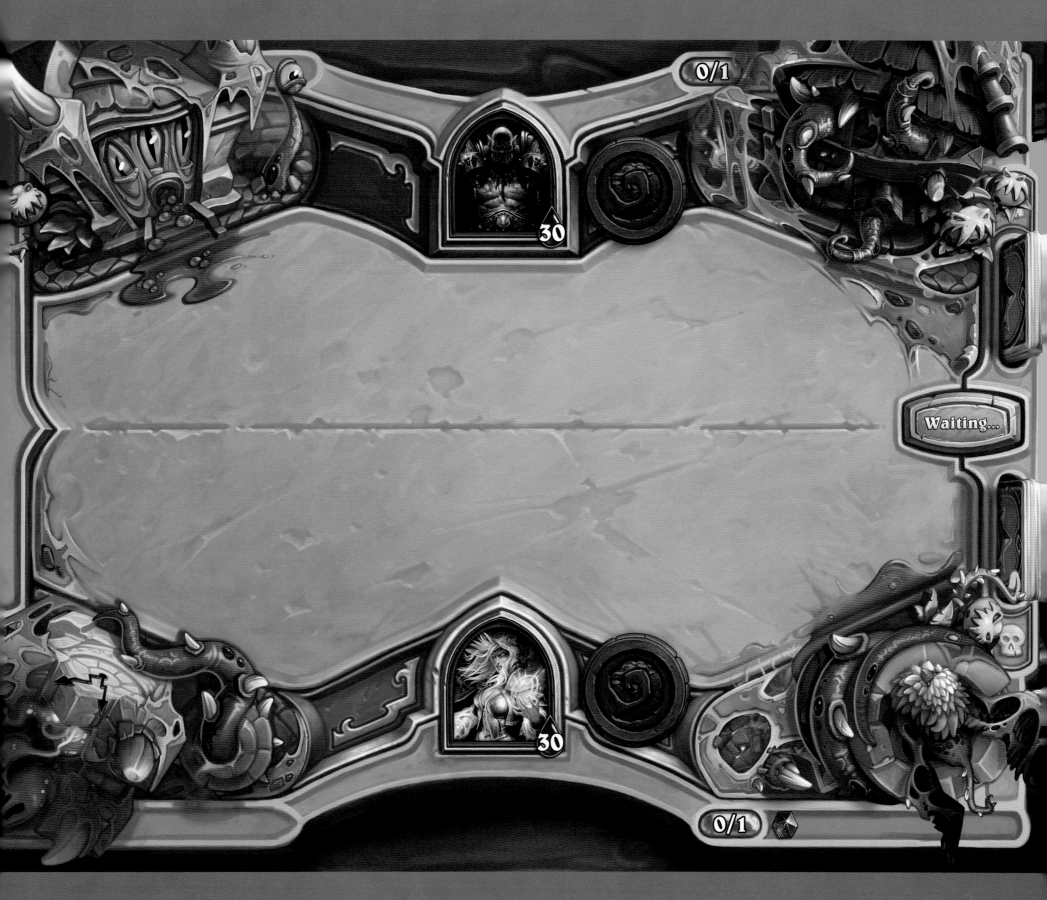

0/1

30

Waiting...

30

0/1

ABOVE
Whispers of the Old Gods pack tray sketch

LEFT
Final *Whispers of the Old Gods* pack tray

OPPOSITE
Whispers of the Old Gods card pack ideation and final art

1 Pack	2 Packs	7 Packs	15 Packs	40 Packs	60 Packs
⊕ 100	$2.99	$9.99	$19.99	$49.99	$69.99

ABOVE
Yogg-Saron, Hope's End
Tooth

ABOVE
Y'Shaarj, Rage Unbound
Samwise Didier

ABOVE
N'Zoth, the Corruptor
Tyson Murphy

ABOVE
C'Thun
James Ryman

ABOVE
Evolve Spines
Alex Alexandrov

OPPOSITE
Call of the Wild
Peter Stapleton

ABOVE
Psych-o-Tron
Matt Dixon

ABOVE
Spawn of N'Zoth
Peter Stapleton

ABOVE
Silver Hand Murloc
Andrew Hou

ABOVE
Vilefin Inquisitor
Jerry Mashcho

ABOVE
Ragnaros, Lightlord
James Ryman

OPPOSITE
Validated Doomsayer
Dany Orizio

ABOVE
Fandral Staghelm
Anton Zemskov

Hallazeal the Ascended
Wayne Reynolds

Darkshire Librarian
Rafael Zanchetin

ABOVE
Herald Volazj
Luke Mancini

ABOVE
Undercity Huckster
Jon Neimeister

ABOVE
Evolved Kobold
Genevieve Tsai and Nutchapol Thitinunthankorn

OPPOSITE
DOOM!
Raymond Swanland

ABOVE
Corrupted Seer
Ryan Metcalf

ABOVE
Flamewreathed Faceless
E.M. Gist

ABOVE
Blade of C'Thun
Steve Prescott

OPPOSITE
Power Word: Tentacles
Jesper Ejsing

Darkshire Councilman
Garrett Hanna

Polluted Hoarder
Matt Dixon

ABOVE
Eternal Sentinel
Jonboy Meyers and Nutchapol Thitinunthankorn

ABOVE
Possessed Villager
Matt Dixon

53

OPPOSITE
Hogger, Doom of Elwynn
Matt Dixon

RIGHT
Bog Creeper
Matt Dixon

3

one night in **Karazhan**™

PRACTICE KARAOKE LIKE JARAXXUS!

—Lord Jaraxxus

A SPECIAL INVITATION

If *Whispers of the Old Gods* had been the darkest *Hearthstone* expansion to date, the next release was to be the silliest. By a wide margin.

One of the most popular encounters in *World of Warcraft* was *Karazhan*, a raid filled with ghostly partygoers, demonic bosses, and a challenging chess game. The tower was a haunted reminder of the tragic fall of the Last Guardian, Medivh.

In lore, Azeroth was silently protected for thousands of years by the Guardian of Tirisfal, a powerful mage chosen to serve as the front line of defense against demonic incursions. When one Guardian fell, another rose in their place. They were recruited for their unwavering dedication and total focus. Medivh's story was one of inevitable tragedy; he struggled with a dark fate and ultimately fell to corruption, unleashing terrible evil upon the humans of Azeroth.

But that wasn't the tone the Hearthstone team was interested in.

What if this adventure took place long before Medivh fell to darkness and tried to destroy the world? He didn't earn the Guardian's power; he was born with it. And maybe, just maybe . . . there was a time in his life when he didn't take the responsibility as seriously as he should have. What would the Hearthstone version of that look like?

PREVIOUS PAGE
Laurel Austin

RIGHT
Mike Azevedo

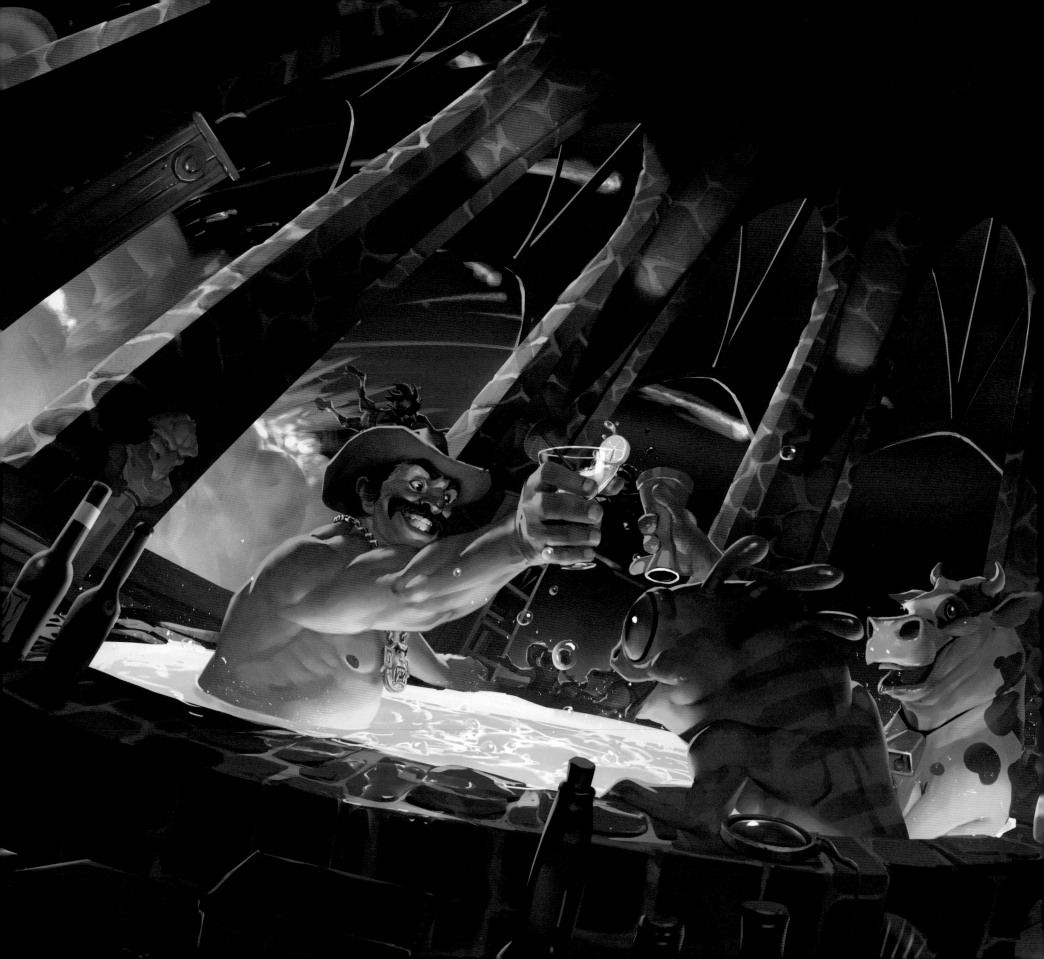

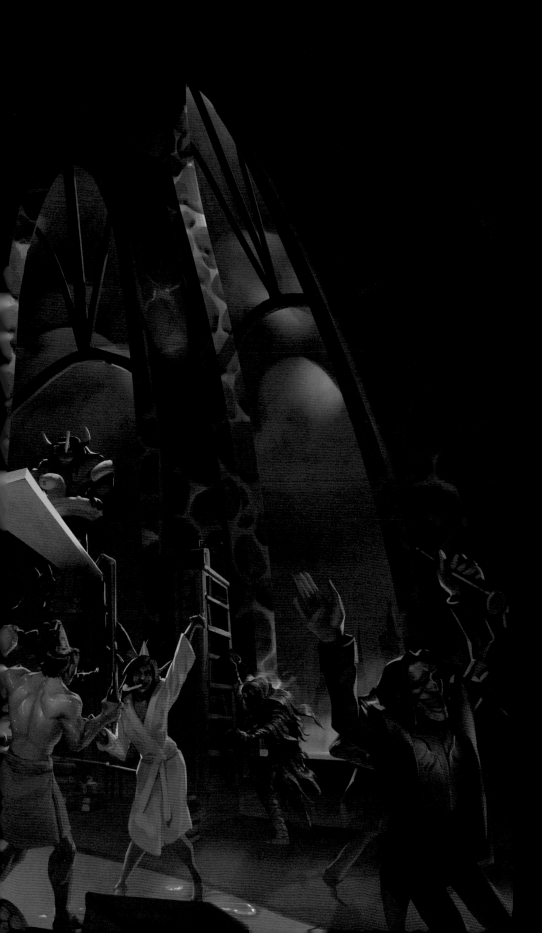

Perhaps Karazhan was home to the most insane parties the world had ever seen, like it was Azeroth's version of Studio 54. After all, the foreboding, haunted interior of Karazhan was filled with dining halls and ballrooms and the tormented spirits of those that once enjoyed it in better days.

Blizzard's cinematics team developed a disco-fueled pitch to imagine those better days, complete with funky beats, laser-lit dancefloors, and magical jacuzzies. It was an instant hit with the Hearthstone development team.

"No joke, I literally didn't know we were allowed to do that," said Jeremy Cranford. "It was great. It was the silliest thing we had ever done at that time. Funny enough, it's sort of the baseline of silliness now. We're expected to go that far."

One Night in Karazhan became the craziest reimagining of Warcraft's lore the Hearthstone team had ever attempted.

Your host, the great magus Medivh invites you back to party down . . . with me!

—MEDIVH

AN ENCHANTED EVENING

The insane cinematic had set the bar high for a late-night legendary party at all levels of the tower of Karazhan. The individual boss encounters in the adventure were heavily inspired by the bosses in the original *World of Warcraft* instance, only with a tremendous number of disco lights, spoiled socialites, and partying demons to contend with.

Building those missions helped the team define exactly what the limitations of silliness should be. Forcing players to dance their minions between suspiciously disco-colored lasers to defeat a boss? Awesome! Having the demon antagonist, **Prince Malchezzar**, argue about party invitations in one of the missions? More, please!

But an early version of *One Night in Karazhan*'s game board showed what "too far" looked like. It was going to commit fully to being a dancefloor, with every corner packed in with Azeroth-inspired nightclub fare. It didn't look enough like Karazhan, so it was reworked to contain a lot more of the tower's iconic locations.

The design and art teams quickly realized that putting too much of the party in the card art itself (or the voice lines associated with it) would feel very odd as time went by. Two or three expansions later, if certain cards would come in with a thumping music intro or art filled with disco lights, it would stick out in a potentially obnoxious way.

The art team found a matching lighthearted tone through different techniques. Several classic characters from Karazhan, like **Barnes** and **Moroes**, were illustrated with a noticeably more cartoonish expressions and proportions than their debut in *World of Warcraft*, though they weren't given any 70s-inspired attire or gaudy party favors. Partygoers like the **Gadgetzan Socialite** wore bright colors and flashy clothes that fit more into a fantasy universe, and new cards, like **Babbling Book** or the absurd **Silverware Golem**, brought some inspiration from classic animated shows and films to the set.

LEFT
Max Grecke and Laurel Austin

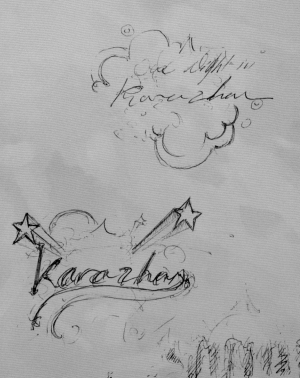

ABOVE
One Night in Karazhan logo ideation and final logo

OPPOSITE
One Night in Karazhan game board

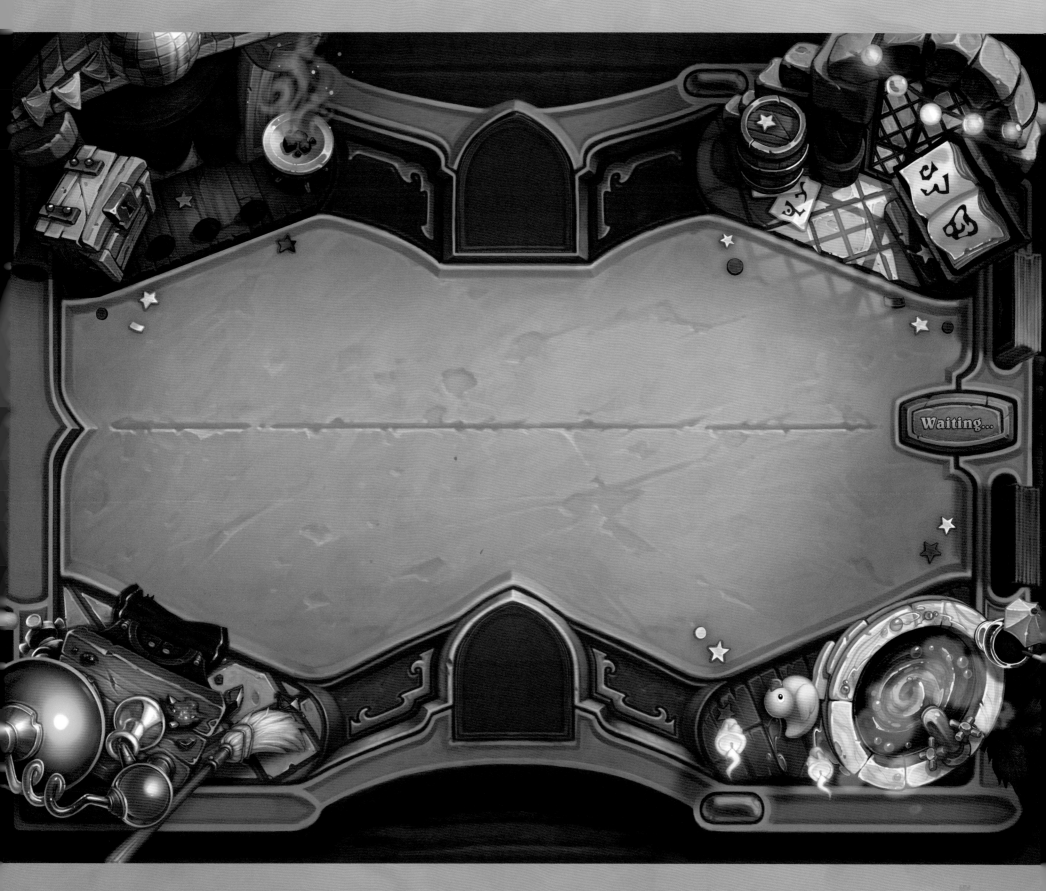

Waiting...

Il Logo and Velvet Background

Light and Confettis

Disco Ball

Cocktail

Wax Seal

Il Logo

THIS SPREAD
One Night in Karazhan
card back sketches

Portal

Wax Seal and Parchment Background

Medivh's Invitation
Charlene Le Scanff

THIS SPREAD
Jomaro Kindred
and Charlene Le Scanff

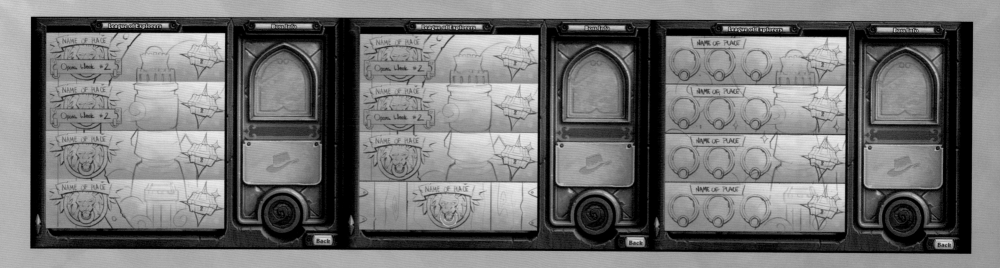

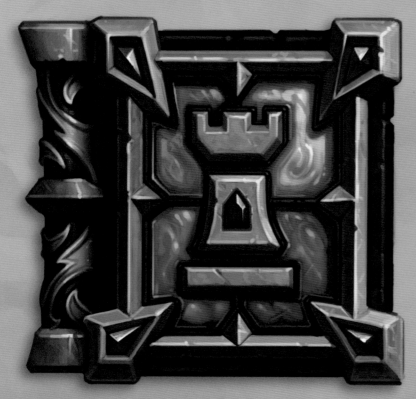

LEFT PAGE
Various user interface sketches elements designed
for the *One Night in Karazhan* expansion

OPPOSITE
Haywire Mech!
Skan Srisuwan

You are cordially invited
to party down at my ultra
sweet magic tower thing.

ABOVE
Ivory Knight
Zoltan Boros

ABOVE
Babbling Book
A.J. Nazzaro

77

OPPOSITE
Menagerie Warden
Alex Horley

RIGHT
Wicked Witchdoctor
Rafael Zanchetin

ABOVE
Swashburglar
Zoltan Boros

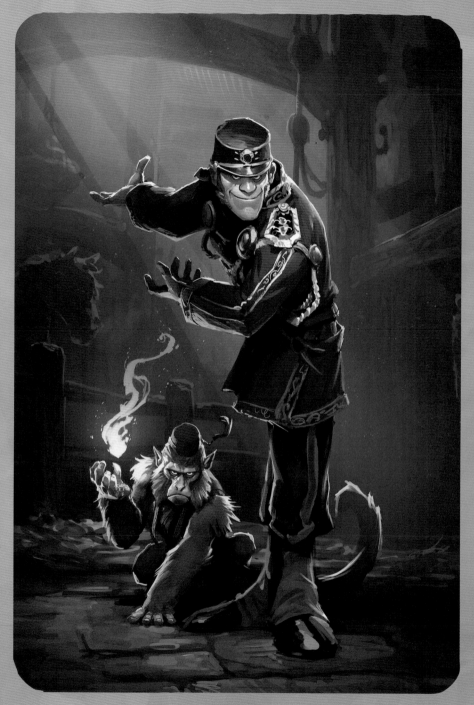

ABOVE
Medivh's Valet
Sean McNally

ABOVE
Moroes
Sean McNally

ABOVE
Barnes
Garrett Hanna

ABOVE
Book Wyrm
Dave Allsop

OPPOSITE
Moat Lurker
Jerry Mascho

ABOVE
Enchanted Raven
Daria Tuzova

ABOVE
Terestian Illhoof
Matt Cavotta

ABOVE
Nightbane
Laurel Austin

OPPOSITE
Prince Malchezaar
Grace Liu and Joe Madureira

ABOVE
Spoon
Genevieve Tsai and Konstantin Turovec

ABOVE
Knife
Genevieve Tsai and Konstantin Turovec

ABOVE
Fork
Genevieve Tsai and Konstantin Turovec

ABOVE
Cup
Ludo Lullabi and C. Luechaiwattasopon

ABOVE
Set the Table
Ludo Lullabi and Akkapoj Thawornsathitwong

OPPOSITE
Pour a Round
Ludo Lullabi and Akkapoj Thawornsathitwong

ABOVE
Medivh, the Guardian
James Ryman

ABOVE
Atiesh
James Ryman

OPPOSITE
Dorothee
Adam Byrne

4

MEAN STREETS OF GADGETZAN™

Hey, join the Goons!
Or meet my fist!

—DON HAN'CHO

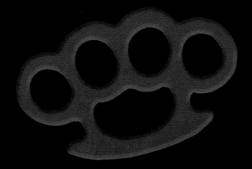

WELCOME TO THE BIG TIME, PAL

If *One Night in Karazhan* had been a reimagining of Azeroth's past, the third and final release of the Year of the Kraken was an interpretation of a possible future.

The small town of Gadgetzan was a lone oasis of greed in the barren desert of Tanaris, but thanks to an unruly dragon and an event known as the Cataclysm, it eventually became a small coastal town. Mayor Noggenfogger would tell you he planned it that way all along.

Now with access to sea trade, that tiny little town suddenly became a valuable port between Azeroth's continents without any of that annoying baggage that comes with faction allegiance or any sort of regulation whatsoever. It's easy to imagine how over the years, a vast number of completely legitimate and not-at-all illegal business folks would take a liking to that sort of environment.

A few years down the line, that little town in the desert could be bursting at the seams. That might lead to disagreements. And with no real laws to restrain them, some folks might form "organizations" to enforce their own rules. That's when we arrive at *Mean Streets of Gadgetzan*—and the alley-fought battles between three crime families for control of Gadgetzan's lucrative (but definitely totally legal, don't question it) business.

PREVIOUS PAGE
Laurel Austin

RIGHT
Justin Thavirat

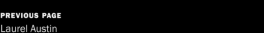

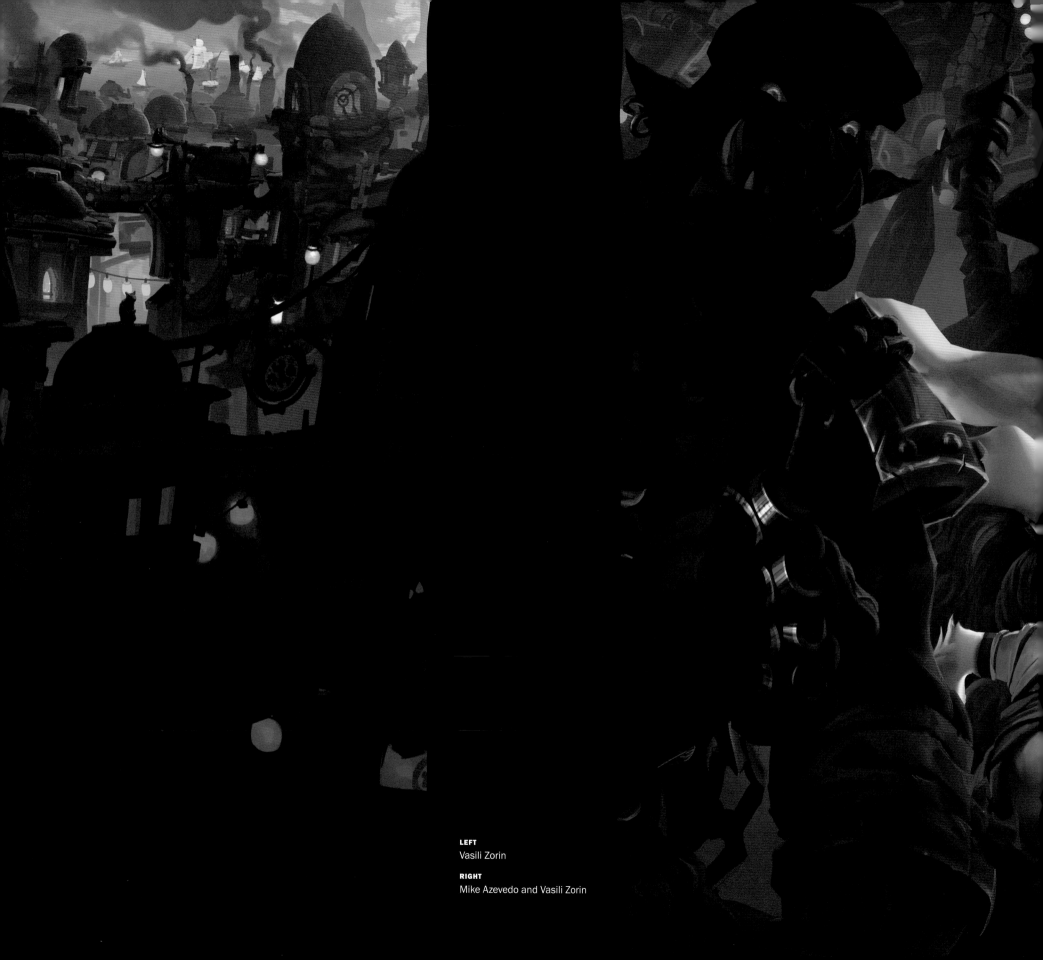

LEFT
Vasili Zorin

RIGHT
Mike Azevedo and Vasili Zorin

While the first expansion of the year was dark, and the second release was absurd, this third release tried to strike a balance in tone, depicting dangerous criminals without getting too serious about it.

"Criminal gangs really aren't that much of a fun thing in real life," said Ben Thompson. "We needed to make sure we hit the right mark."

Certain tropes that go with Prohibition-era gangsters—pinstripe suits, matching fedoras, brass knuckles, and oversized bodyguards—were perfect.

Others, like automatic machine guns, didn't feel right in Warcraft or Hearthstone. *The Mean Streets of Gadgetzan* cinematic has a Tommy gun or two, but when it came to the cards and characters in the set, the designers took a different approach—for example, hunters can carry a gun, but it shoots piranhas, not bullets.

It was a good start. The art team was on its way to make turf wars as fun as they could possibly be.

Ah, Gadgetzan!
The city of opportunity!

—Cinematic Trailer

Welcome to the big time, pal!

—CINEMATIC TRAILER

THEY COME IN THREES

Each of *Hearthstone*'s nine classes were matched with one of the three criminal organizations. Warriors, paladins, and hunters joined the brawny Grimy Goons; druids, rogues, and shaman teamed up with the golem-spawning Jade Lotus; and mages, priests, and warlocks signed up with the reckless spellcasters of the Kabal.

Each crime family had its own selection of tri-class cards, which often let players **Discover** cards from other classes for the first time.

Previously, the Hearthstone team's designers had been restricted to developing cards for one class or all classes. Now they had a middle ground. They could create a card like **Kazakus** without having to worry about what would happen if a rogue player used **Shadowstep** on it. Twice.

The tri-class grouping meant each gang needed to be instantly recognizable and distinctive from the others, and that meant the Hearthstone team needed to figure out exactly who these gangs were and what characters would lead them.

Mean Streets of Gadgetzan was the first time the art team developed an expansion-wide "style guide," which helped define not only the three crime families but how their territories should look.

"Gadgetzan needed to look big and overgrown. We stacked the buildings on top of each other and made them look unsafe," said concept artist Charlene Le Scanff. "And if you look closely, you can see we always tried to imagine that each building was part of a gang's territory, so they were each designed and decorated differently."

Special attention was also given to the different crime families' choice of weapons to make sure each group felt unique and cohesive. The Goons had their goofy guns and bludgeons, the Jade Lotus had an affinity for sleek blades, and the Kabal had a fondness for wands and magical instruments.

Those same visual guidelines also helped influence the expansion's game board, which featured buildings from each crime family on the corners of the board.

ABOVE
Wooden expansion sign

RIGHT
Jomaro Kindred

OPPOSITE
Mean Streets of Gadgetzan
logo ideation and final logo

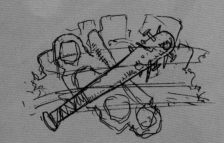

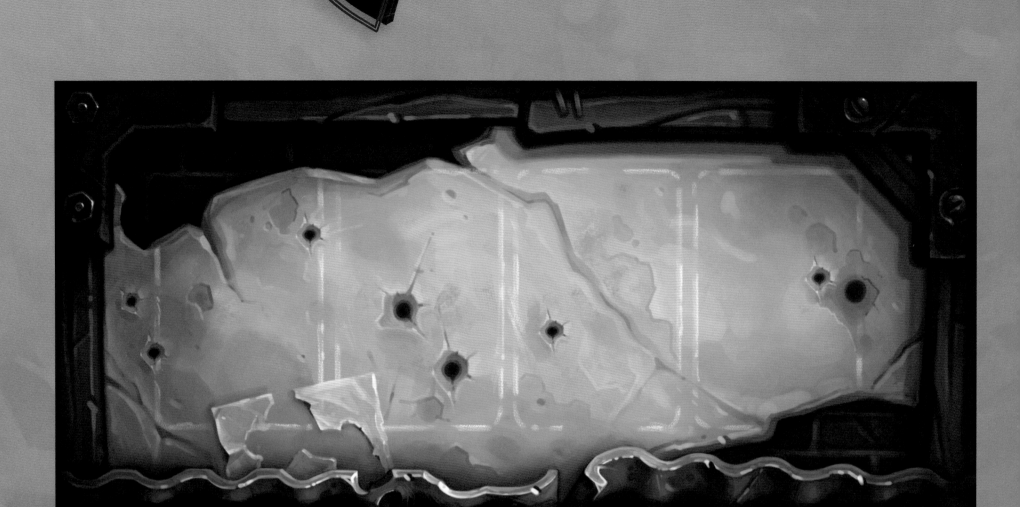

ABOVE
Mean Streets of Gadgetzan card pack tray

OPPOSITE
Mean Streets of Gadgetzan game board

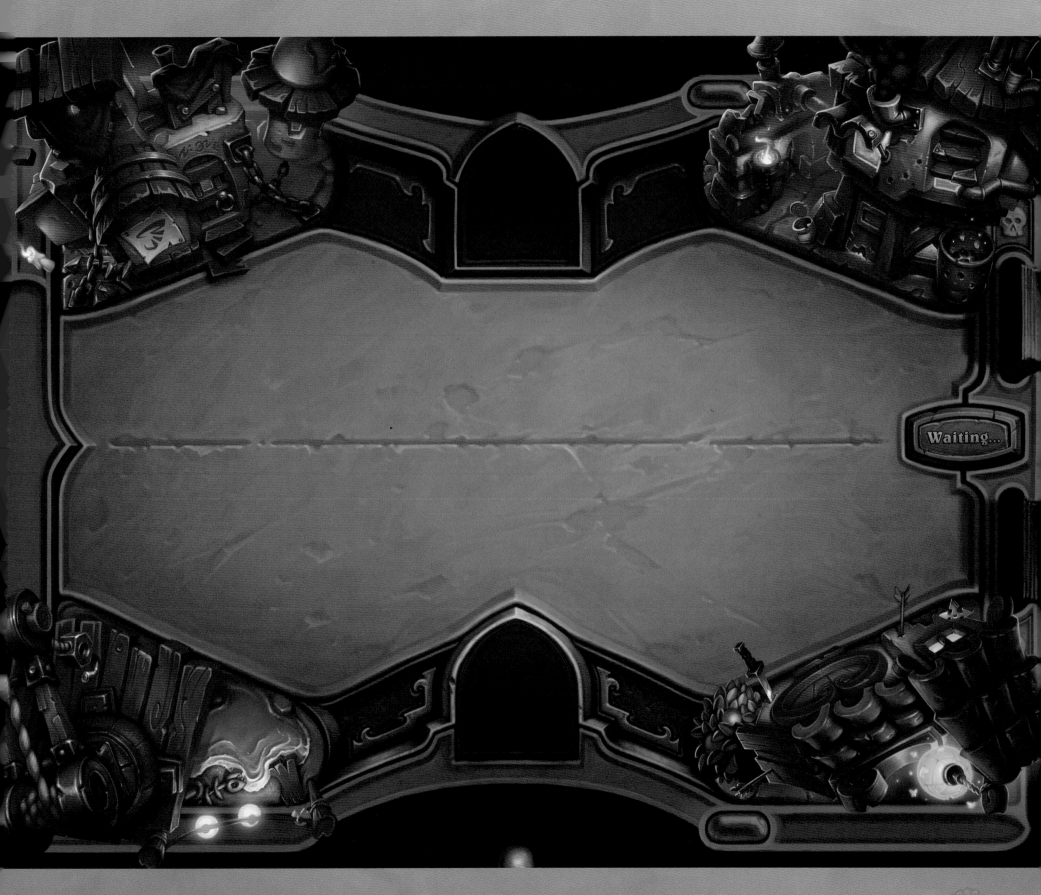

Waiting...

M.OBSTERS

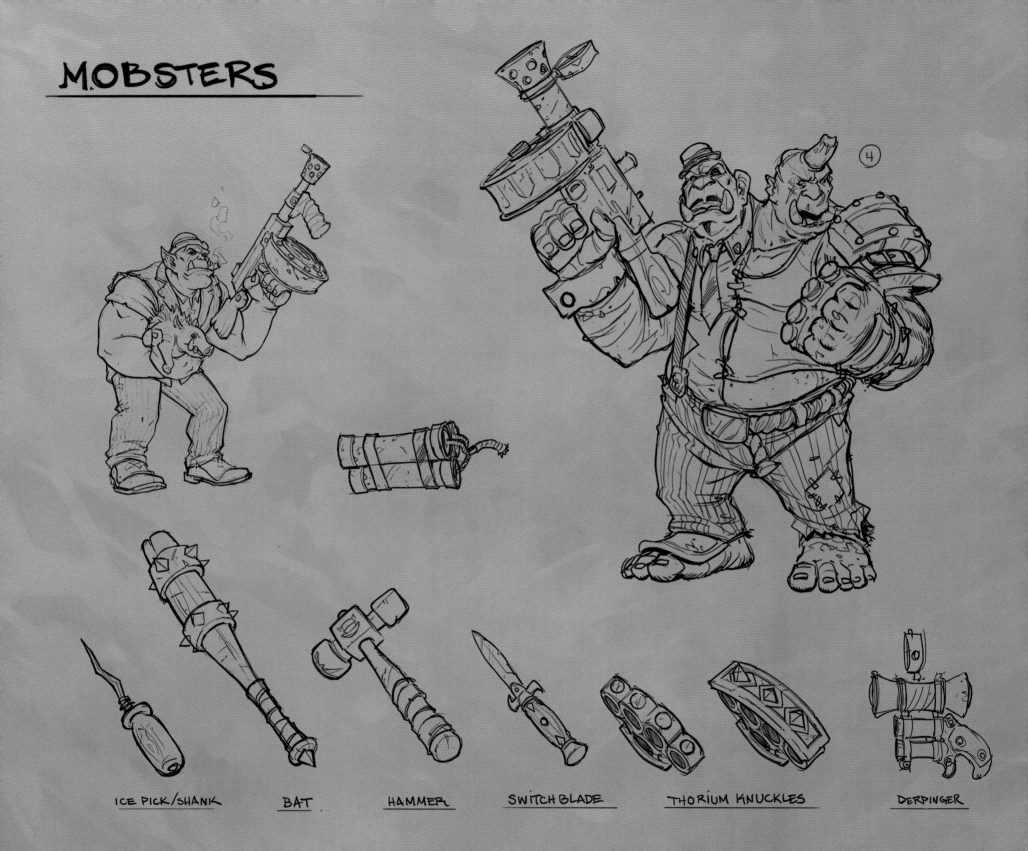

ICE PICK/SHANK   BAT   HAMMER   SWITCHBLADE   THORIUM KNUCKLES   DERPINGER

THIS SPREAD
Jomaro Kindred

PIRANHA GUN

(ORC) ROCK SPITTER

THE GRIMY GOONS

If you need any help in the art of extortion, robbery, battery, intimidation, witness "rehabilitation," or any other muscle-based activities, give a call to the Grimy Goons. And you will call them, if you know what's good for you.

The Grimy Goons were the first crime family to find its strong visual identity. Once the art team settled on the idea of having their leader, **Don Han'Cho**, be a two-headed ogre, everything locked into place. **Don Han'Cho** managed to pack both brains and brawn into one ill-matched package. The physically powerful races of Warcraft—like the orcs, goblins, and tauren—were prime candidates for recruitment, and **Don Han'Cho** ran them exactly the way you'd expect: Poorly.

As the game design team began to give the Goons some powerful hand-buff mechanics that could pump up minions to herculean proportions, the art team gave them the backstory of weapon smugglers who could arm anyone with some extra firepower. This crew is almost the purest visual realization of the initial idea for *Mean Streets of Gadgetzan*: Cartoon gangsters causing indiscriminate mayhem.

THE JADE LOTUS

The black market has never looked so good. When you need something exotic, dangerous, and stolen, you call the elegant thieves and assassins of the Jade Lotus. Always remember: You can't make an omelet without breaking a few faces.

It took some iteration, but the art team slowly began to develop the identity for Gadgetzan's second crime family, the Jade Lotus. Unlike the brass knuckle-carrying Grimy Goons, the Jade Lotus worked in the shadows, focusing on silent eliminations rather than open street brawls. Their members were drawn mostly from the creatures seen on the continent of Pandaria, and their leader became one of the team's favorite characters.

Aya Blackpaw is a hyperactive, short, lethal pandaren with a hulking, silent bodyguard named **White Eyes**. Though her crew has all the skills they need to remain unseen, she just can't resist hurling out her army of jade golems.

JADE FOO DOG MASK

(EXPLORER'S HAT)

THIS SPREAD
Jomaro Kindred

SHADOW TOTEM

JADE LOTUS

SHADOW TOTEM

KAXXI

THIS SPREAD
Jomaro Kindred

MURLOC NINJA

VERMIN/BRAWLERS

JINYU

115

MANA HORNS

THE KABAL

You don't need a normal potion. You don't even need a safe potion. Your problems are bigger than that. That's where the Kabal comes in. For just a few coins and a few ounces of your soul (which you probably weren't using anyway), they'll concoct exactly what you need to solve your problems. No refunds.

Early in Gadgetzan's development, the design team knew they wanted to have a magic-based crime family, but finding the exact implementation of that was a bit tricky. Once concept artists put a face to the leader of the spell-slinging Kabal, the whole idea began to make more sense: He was a crazed-looking troll named Kazakus, brewing potions of dubious usefulness . . . who also just happens to be a dragon in disguise.

The original plan was to have **Kazakus's** mechanic involve transforming him into a monstrously dangerous dragon after he entered play, but not too long before the game launched, the design team decided on something different. **Kazakus's** new power was to brew a custom potion, which would allow players to construct what they needed to win the match.

Each of those possibilities required a different piece of art to represent the potion. With all the different options, almost forty different pieces of art were needed just for that one card.

The overall look of the Kabal required some extra work from the concept art team. *Whispers of the Old Gods* had shown off a number of cultist cards only a few months earlier, so the magical enforcers of the Kabal needed to look different than that.

"It ended up being an easy solution," said Jeremy Cranford. "All of the cultists wore hoods and cloaks. We gave the Kabal cowls instead. It worked great."

BARBER SHOP

THIS SPREAD
Environmental iteration

NEXT PAGE
Charlene Le Scanff

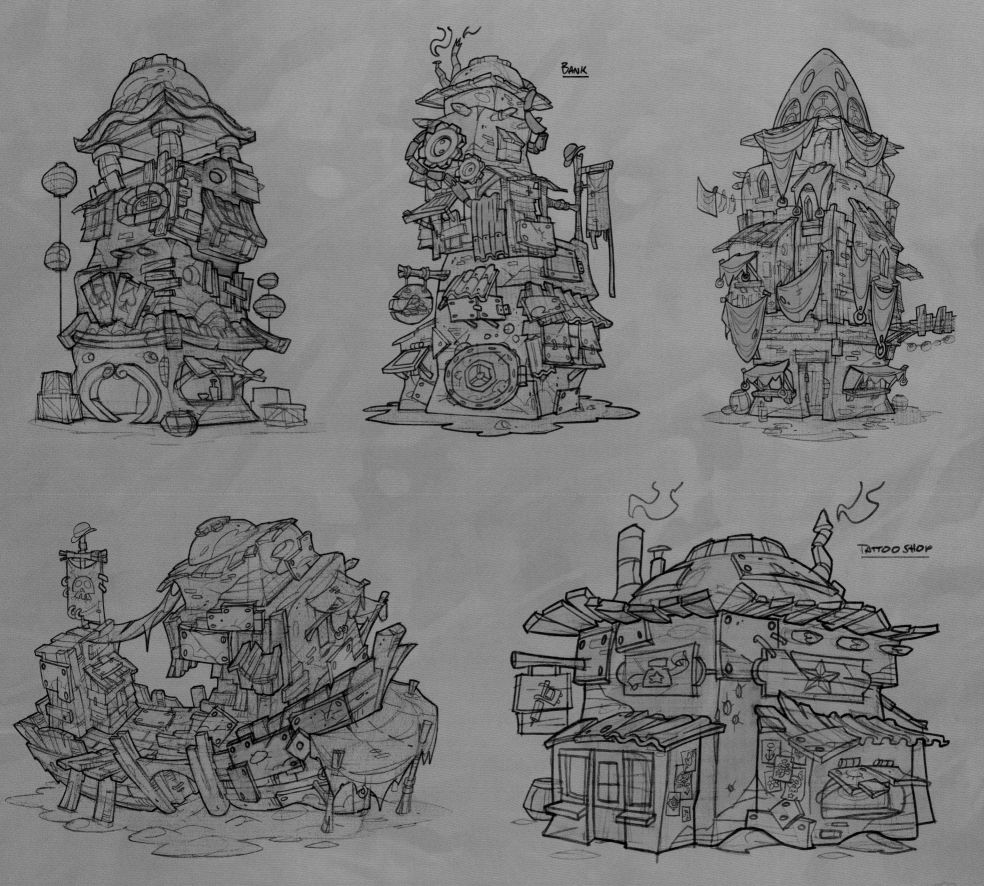

BANK

TATTOO SHOP

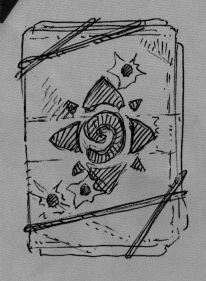

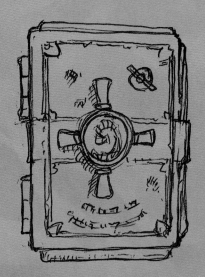
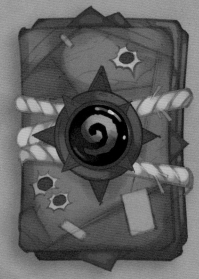

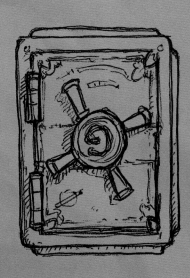

THIS SPREAD
Mean Streets of Gadgetzan card pack and opening mechanism ideation, and final card pack

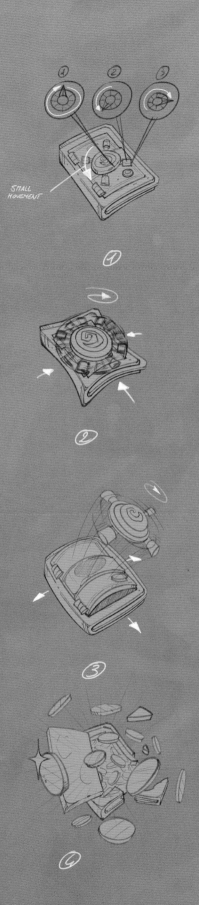

SMALL
MOVEMENT

potion

THIS SPREAD
Konstantin Turovec

124

ABOVE
Drakonid Operative
Zoltan Boros

ABOVE
Shaky Zipgunner
Andrew Hou

ABOVE
Gadgetzan Ferryman
Zoltan Boros

ABOVE
Dirty Rat
Orci Nomine Veritatis

ABOVE
Piranha
Nick Southham

OPPOSITE
Piranha Launcher
Nick Southham

ABOVE
Patches the Pirate
James Ryman

ABOVE
Jade Golem
Konstantin Turovec

ABOVE
Abyssal Enforcer
Luke Mancini

ABOVE
Kazakus
Jomaro Kindred

ABOVE
Cryomancer
Tyler West Studios

ABOVE
Hozen Healer
Sam Nielson

ABOVE
Counterfeit Coin
Joe Wilson

OPPOSITE
Aya Blackpaw
Glenn Rane

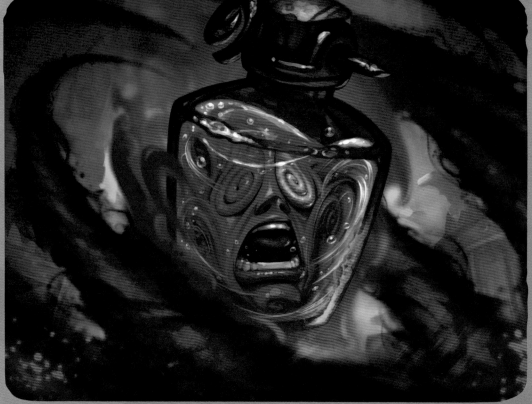

LEFT ABOVE
Mark of the Lotus
Wayne Reynolds

LEFT BOTTOM
Potion of Madness
Arthur Bozonnet

OPPOSITE
Lunar Visions
Arthur Bozonnet

ABOVE
Worgen Greaser
Alex Alexandrov

ABOVE
Sergeant Sally
Matt Dixon

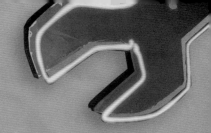

ABOVE
Spiked Hogrider
Mike Sass

OPPOSITE
Dragonfire Potion
Charlene Le Scanff

ABOVE
Finja, the Flying Star
Matt Dixon

ABOVE
Smuggler's Run
Alex Horley

OPPOSITE
White Eyes
Cole Eastburn

ABOVE
Grimscale Chum
Matt Dixon

ABOVE
Wickerflame Burnbristle
Matt Dixon

5

THE TAVERN GROWS

Let's have some fun!

—Nemsy Necrofizzle

TAVERN BRAWLS AND FIRESIDE GATHERINGS

Many years ago, the first prototypes of *Hearthstone* were played on paper. Two developers sat across from each other with physical cards, face to face, and squared off. When the game became playable in a digital format, those early years were filled with internal playtests with people in the same room.

Shortly after *Hearthstone*'s announcement in 2013, Blizzard began its company-wide playtest, opening it up to several thousand players who rarely played in the same room—but even that version had a closely knit social component because it would show the other employee's real name and not their Battle.net ID. Most matches were followed by post-match discussions and connections through the company's instant messenger.

The full, public release of the game could never have that level of a personal connection. The internet is an anonymous place, after all, for better or for worse.

But the game team never forgot how much fun a game of *Hearthstone* could be when you were physically sitting across from your opponent. And they never stopped building features that would encourage people to gather in public to sling some cards together.

"This sounds corny, but it's true: Being around other people matters," said lead designer Pat Nagle. "The game plays differently. It's fun in a completely different way."

One of the most notable features began as the Tavern Brawl mode which first released in mid-2015. Every week, for a limited time, players are matched up with unusual rulesets, ranging from randomized pre-built decks, to high-risk, high-reward deckbuilding challenges, and even to cooperative games where the two players would work together to defeat an AI opponent.

Hearthstone team artists even created a special aesthetic for the Tavern Brawl. Upon firing up the Tavern Brawl, players are greeted with a chalkboard-style sketch that riffs on the rules and invites players in to check it out.

This mode is largely played online between randomly matched players, but designers quickly began to prototype Tavern Brawls that could only be played in person. Some of these modes involved rules that required verbal communication, while others even asked multiple players to gather around a single device. There were modes where an entire crowd would individually pitch in for an assault on a boss character, and others where players could compete against each other using decks created by *Hearthstone* world champions!

These exclusive modes are called Fireside Brawls and can only be played at events called Fireside Gatherings. These are the essence of the social fun of *Hearthstone*. A host picks a real-life location, registers it with Blizzard, and invites all local players to come out for a few hours of friendly competition and exclusive rewards. And as the years have passed, the Hearthstone team has released more and more art that innkeepers can use to decorate their events, from an online tavern sign creator to stylized "quest logs," from to printable tournament lists to bingo cards.

The biggest Fireside Gathering in the world is BlizzCon each year, but there are many smaller ones popping up all over the globe.

FIRESIDE GATHERING

Pull up a chair and join us for our local Hearthstone meet up. It's free, incredibly fun, and you'll earn a special card back just for participating!

Location

Date/Time   Contact Us

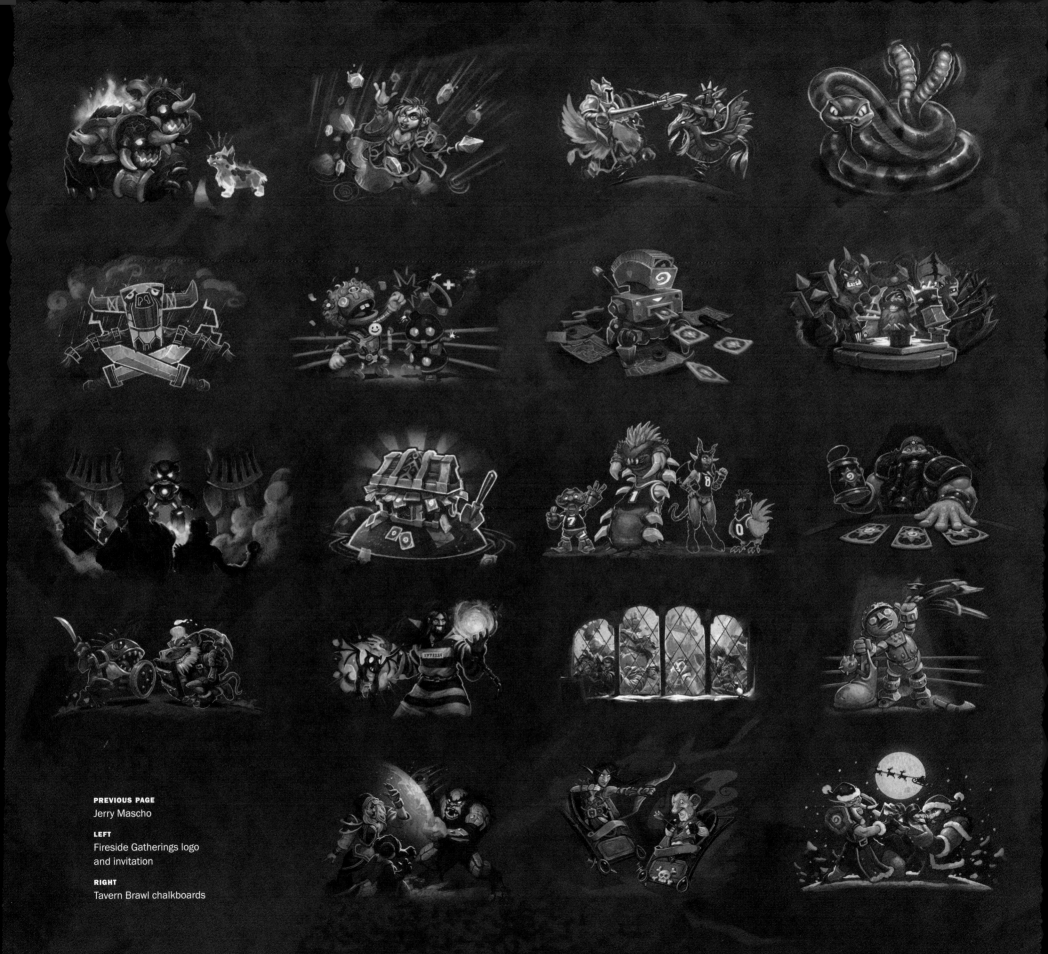

PREVIOUS PAGE
Jerry Mascho

LEFT
Fireside Gatherings logo
and invitation

RIGHT
Tavern Brawl chalkboards

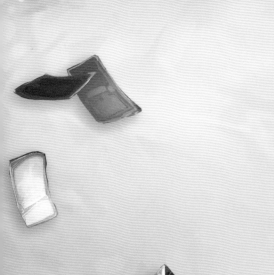

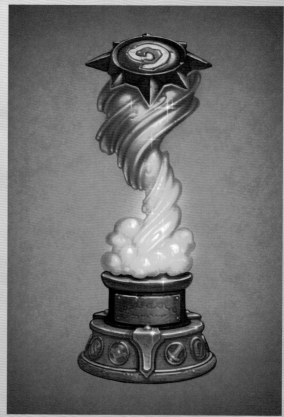

Compass Rose is tilted at roughly 45 deg.

Beadblasted/Frosted or otherwise matte finish tinted glass. Ideally the color tint would fade from light to dark.

Aged wood. Think: hard used/burnished tavern table

All metal is a beaten warm tinted pewter or similar metal

The Glass extends through the base of the trophy and sockets the Compass rose to the top. The end effect is a glowing magical swirl of mana when the trophy is set atop a lit pedastal

ABOVE
Hearthstone esports trophy concept art

RIGHT
Hearthstone esports trophy design process

The kraken had its fun, didn't it?
Caused a little mayhem, threw a party,
and let loose an army of jade golems.
That last bit took some effort to clean up,
but I've seen worse in my days. Like this one
time, long ago, I accidentally dropped a mug
of my finest brew on a gryphon's head, and
she was so mad that she spread her wings
and raised her talons and . . .

Well, that's not really important.

But after a year, the kraken went back to
the depths to slumber again. (I think it might
enjoyed Medivh's shindig just a wee bit too
much.) And when it did, I saw the stars
change once again.

Something new was coming.
Something **mammoth** in size . . .

—Harth Stonebrew, the Innkeeper

Fireside
Ben Thompson

Welcome Inn
Charlene Le Scanff

Jade Lotus
Jomaro Kindred

Zul'Drak
Charlene Le Scanff

Tauren
Charlene LeScanff

Eyes of C'Thun
Jomaro Kindred

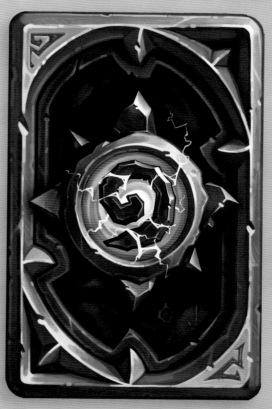

Kabal
Charlene Le Scanff

Hogger
Jerry Mascho

Grimy Goons
Jerry Mascho

Tyrande
Charlene Le Scanff

Secret Level
Ben Thompson

Clutch of Yogg-Saron
Jomaro Kindred

Legion
Charlene Le Scanff

Medivh's Invitation
Charlene Le Scanff

Tinyfin Beach
Charlene Le Scanff

The Blue Portal
Charlene Le Scanff

Karazhan Nights
Charlene Le Scanff

Pie
Charlene Le Scanff

Shadowmoon Valley
Charlene Le Scanff

Year of the Kraken card back sketch
Jerry Masho

Halfhill
Charlene Le Scanff

Year of the Kraken
Jerry Mascho

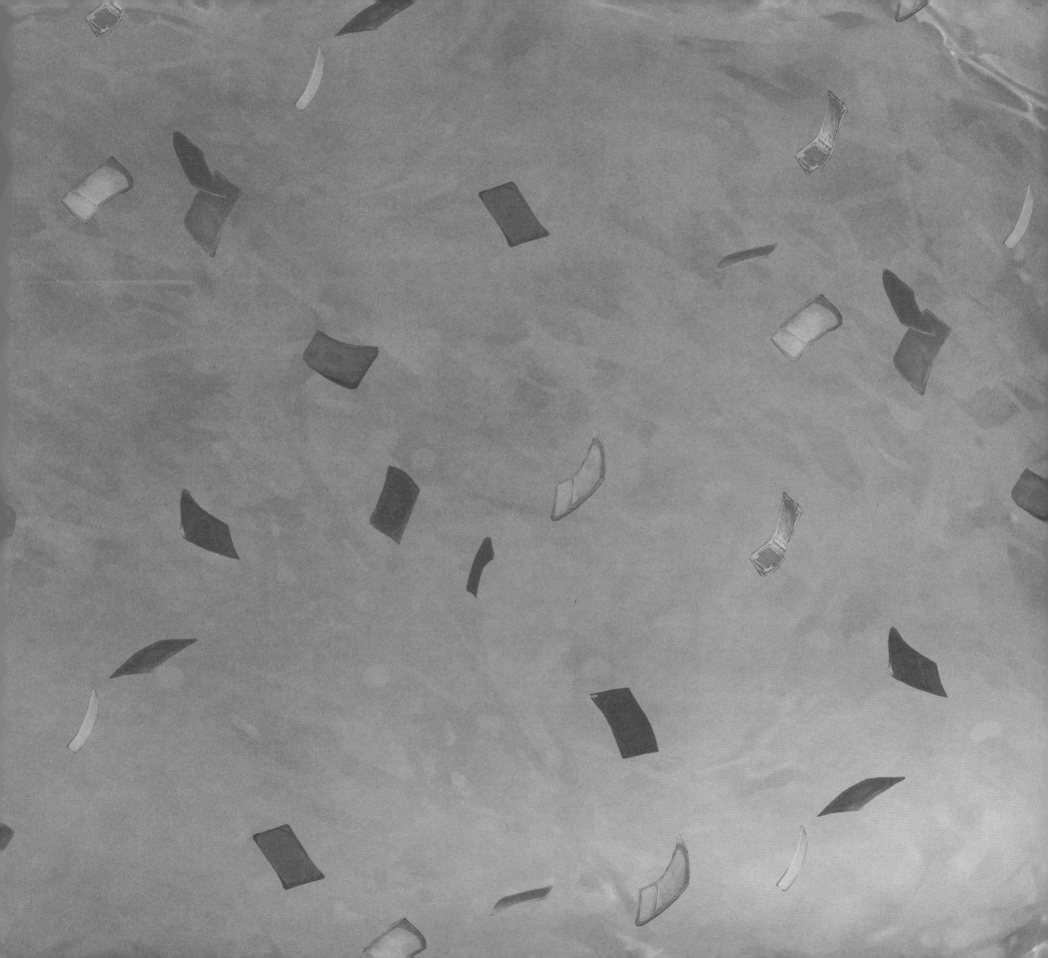